I0490971

Contents

Introduction

Chapter 1: Types of Affiliate Marketing

Chapter 2: Pay-Per-Sale (PPS)

Chapter 3: Pay-Per-Lead (PPL)

Chapter 4: Pay-Per-Click (PPC)

Chapter 5: Cost-Per-Action (CPA)

Chapter 6: Revenue Sharing

Chapter 7: Cost-Per-Impression (CPM)

Introduction

Affiliate marketing is a performance-based marketing strategy where a business rewards affiliates for each customer brought about by the affiliate's own marketing efforts. The affiliate earns a commission for every sale made through their unique referral link. Affiliate marketing is a win-win scenario for both the business and the affiliate, as the business benefits from increased sales and exposure, while the affiliate earns a commission for their efforts.

The basic concept of affiliate marketing is simple: a business partners with affiliates who promote their products or services. In return for their promotional efforts, the affiliates earn a commission on any resulting sales. The commission can be a percentage of the sale, a flat fee, or even a combination of the two. The affiliate's role is to attract customers to the business's website and convince them to make a purchase.

Affiliate marketing is one of the most cost-effective forms of online marketing, as the business only pays the affiliate when a sale is made. This means that the business does not have to pay for expensive advertising campaigns upfront, and instead, can focus on rewarding affiliates for their successful marketing efforts.

To get started with affiliate marketing, a business needs to find and partner with affiliates. This can be done through a variety of methods, including online affiliate networks, affiliate management agencies, or even directly contacting affiliates. The business should also have a clear understanding of their target audience and the products or services they are promoting, as well as an efficient system in place for tracking and paying commissions to affiliates.

One of the biggest benefits of affiliate marketing is the ability to reach a large, targeted audience. Affiliates can reach customers through a variety of channels, including their own websites, social media, email lists, and more. The ability to reach such a large audience can result in increased sales and exposure for the business, as well as increased commissions for the affiliates.

Another benefit of affiliate marketing is that it allows for a more flexible working arrangement. Affiliates can work from anywhere and at any time, as long as they have a computer and an internet connection. This can be especially advantageous for those who are unable to work a traditional 9-5 job, such as stay-at-home parents or individuals with disabilities.

In conclusion, affiliate marketing is a mutually beneficial relationship between a business and its affiliates. The business benefits from increased sales and exposure, while the affiliates earn a commission for their promotional efforts. With its low costs and the ability to reach a large, targeted audience, affiliate marketing can be a highly effective form of online marketing for both small and large businesses.

Chapter 1: Types of Affiliate Marketing

Pay-per-sale (PPS)

This is one of the most straightforward methods of affiliate marketing, where affiliates earn a commission for each sale made through their referral link. The commission is typically a percentage of the sale, and the affiliate is paid only when the customer makes a purchase. This method is beneficial for businesses, as they only pay for actual sales and do not have to pay for clicks or impressions that do not result in a sale.

Pay-per-lead (PPL)

This method involves affiliates earning a commission for each qualified lead generated through their referral link. A qualified lead is defined as a customer who takes a specific action, such as filling out a form or signing up for a newsletter. This method is commonly used by businesses in industries such as finance or insurance, where the lead has a higher value.

Pay-per-click (PPC)

In this method, affiliates earn a commission for each click on their referral link. The commission is usually a flat fee, and the affiliate is paid regardless of whether the customer makes a purchase. This method is often used by businesses that sell digital products, such as ebooks or online courses, as it allows them to generate sales without having to pay a commission on each sale.

Cost-per-action (CPA)

This method is similar to PPL, where affiliates earn a commission for each qualified action taken by the customer. However, unlike PPL, the commission is typically a flat fee rather than a percentage of the sale. This method is often used by businesses that sell products or services with a high average sale value, as it allows them to reward affiliates for each action taken without having to pay a large commission on each sale.

Revenue sharing

This method involves affiliates earning a percentage of the revenue generated by the customer. The affiliate is typically paid a portion of the revenue for the lifetime of the customer, rather than just on the initial sale. This method is often used by businesses that offer recurring services, such as subscription-based products or services.

Cost-per-impression (CPI)

This method involves affiliates earning a commission for each impression generated by their referral link. An impression is defined as a display of the advertisement on a webpage. This method is commonly used by businesses that sell advertising space, as it allows them to generate revenue from each impression without having to rely on actual sales.

Each of these methods of affiliate marketing can be effective in generating revenue, and the best method will depend on the specific business, products or services being sold, and target audience. It is important for businesses to choose the method that best aligns with their goals and objectives, and to clearly communicate the terms and conditions of the affiliate program to potential affiliates. The following chapters will go into each of these methods in detail to provide you with the detail you need to help you select the correct method.

Chapter 2: Pay-Per-Sale (PPS)

Pay-per-sale (PPS) affiliate marketing is one of the most popular methods of affiliate marketing. With this model, affiliates are rewarded for every sale that they generate through their referral link. When a customer clicks on an affiliate's referral link and makes a purchase, the affiliate earns a commission, which is typically a percentage of the sale.

PPS is a popular method of affiliate marketing because it incentivizes affiliates to drive sales. The more sales an affiliate generates, the more money they can earn. Additionally, businesses only pay for actual sales, which makes this method cost-effective.

In this chapter, we'll explore the PPS affiliate marketing model in more detail, including how it works, the benefits of using this model, and tips for succeeding as a PPS affiliate marketer.

How Pay-Per-Sale Affiliate Marketing Works

In a PPS affiliate marketing program, a business (also known as a merchant) pays affiliates to promote their products or services. The affiliate's role is to drive traffic to the merchant's website and encourage customers to make a purchase. When a customer makes a purchase through the affiliate's referral link, the affiliate earns a commission.

The commission rate varies depending on the product or service being sold and the affiliate program. Some affiliate programs offer a flat commission rate for all products, while others offer higher commission rates for high-ticket items. For example, an affiliate promoting a $1,000 product may earn a 10% commission, which would result in a $100 payout.

To become a PPS affiliate marketer, you'll need to find businesses that offer affiliate programs. There are a few ways to do this:

- Look for businesses in your niche: Start by identifying businesses in your niche that sell products or services that would appeal to your audience. Many businesses have affiliate programs, so you can check their website or reach out to them directly to inquire about their program.
- Use affiliate networks: There are many affiliate networks, such as Commission Junction, ShareASale, and ClickBank, that connect businesses with affiliate marketers. You can sign up for these networks and search for affiliate programs that match your interests.
- Check social media: Many businesses promote their affiliate programs on social media, so you can search for relevant hashtags or follow businesses in your niche to stay updated on affiliate opportunities.

Once you've identified businesses with affiliate programs, you can sign up and start promoting their products or services. Here's how:

Choose the right products or services to promote

To be successful as a PPS affiliate marketer, you need to choose products or services that are relevant to your audience and that you believe in. You should also look for products or services that have a high commission rate and that are in high demand.

Create high-quality content

Your success as a PPS affiliate marketer depends on your ability to drive traffic to the merchant's website. To do this, you'll need to create high-quality content that appeals to your audience. This could be in the form of blog posts, videos, social media posts, or other types of content.

Include your affiliate link

When you promote a product or service, be sure to include your affiliate link. This is the link that the customer will use to make a purchase, and it's how the merchant will track your sales and pay you a commission.

Drive traffic to the merchant's website

Your goal as a PPS affiliate marketer is to drive as much traffic to the merchant's website as possible. You can do this by promoting your content on social media, optimizing your website for search engines, or using paid advertising.

Encourage customers to make a purchase

Finally, your job as a PPS affiliate marketer is to encourage customers to make a purchase. This can be done by providing valuable information about the product or service, highlighting its benefits, and addressing any concerns or objections that the customer may have.

Benefits of Pay-Per-Sale Affiliate Marketing

PPS affiliate marketing offers many benefits to both affiliates and merchants. Here are some of the key benefits:

Cost-effective

With PPS affiliate marketing, businesses only pay for actual sales, which makes it a cost-effective marketing strategy.

Increased sales

PPS affiliate marketing incentivizes affiliates to drive sales, which can lead to increased revenue for businesses.

Low risk

Since businesses only pay for actual sales, there is no risk of paying for ineffective marketing campaigns.

Increased brand exposure

By partnering with affiliates, businesses can increase their brand exposure and reach new audiences.

Diverse marketing channels

With PPS affiliate marketing, businesses can reach customers through a variety of marketing channels, including social media, blogs, and email marketing.

Tips for Succeeding as a Pay-Per-Sale Affiliate Marketer

To succeed as a PPS affiliate marketer, there are a few things you can do to increase your chances of success:

Choose the right products or services to promote

As mentioned earlier, it's important to choose products or services that are relevant to your audience and that have a high commission rate.

Create high-quality content

Your success as a PPS affiliate marketer depends on your ability to drive traffic to the merchant's website. To do this, you'll need to create high-quality content that appeals to your audience.

Build an engaged audience

It's important to build an engaged audience that trusts your recommendations. This can be done by providing valuable information and engaging with your audience through comments and social media.

Use multiple marketing channels

To reach as many potential customers as possible, you should use multiple marketing channels, such as social media, blogs, and email marketing.

Monitor your results

It's important to monitor your results and adjust your strategy as needed. You should track your sales and conversion rates, and make changes to your marketing strategy if you're not seeing the results you want.

Conclusion

Pay-per-sale (PPS) affiliate marketing is a popular method of affiliate marketing that offers many benefits to both affiliates and merchants. With this model, affiliates are rewarded for every sale they generate through their referral link. To succeed as a PPS affiliate marketer, you'll need to choose the right products or services to promote, create high-quality content, build an engaged audience, use multiple marketing channels, and monitor your results. By following these tips, you can increase your chances of success as a PPS affiliate marketer and earn a steady stream of passive income.

Chapter 3: Pay-Per-Lead (PPL)

Pay-per-lead (PPL) affiliate marketing is a popular method of affiliate marketing that rewards affiliates for generating leads for businesses. In this model, affiliates are paid a commission for every lead they generate, which can be a valuable source of passive income. In this chapter, we'll take a closer look at pay-per-lead affiliate marketing, how it works, and how to succeed as a PPL affiliate marketer.

Pay-per-lead affiliate marketing is a type of affiliate marketing where affiliates are rewarded for generating leads for businesses. In this model, businesses pay affiliates a commission for each lead they generate through their referral link. A lead is typically defined as a potential customer who has expressed interest in a product or service, such as by filling out a contact form or signing up for a newsletter.

The commission rate for pay-per-lead affiliate marketing can vary widely depending on the industry and the business. Typically, the commission rate for pay-per-lead affiliate marketing is lower than pay-per-sale affiliate marketing, as businesses are taking on more risk by paying for leads that may not convert into sales. However, PPL affiliate marketing can still be a valuable source of passive income for affiliates who are able to generate a high volume of leads.

Pay-per-lead affiliate marketing works by incentivizing affiliates to generate leads for businesses. Here's how it works:

An affiliate signs up for a PPL affiliate program

As with other types of affiliate marketing, affiliates must first sign up for a pay-per-lead affiliate program to participate. This typically involves filling out an application and being approved by the business.

The affiliate promotes the business's products or services

Once the affiliate is approved, they can begin promoting the business's products or services through their referral link. This may involve creating content, running ads, or using other marketing channels to drive traffic to the business's website.

The customer expresses interest in the product or service

When a potential customer clicks on the affiliate's referral link and expresses interest in the business's product or service, they are taken to a landing page where they can learn more and provide their contact information.

The lead is tracked and attributed to the affiliate

When the customer provides their contact information, the lead is tracked and attributed to the affiliate. The business then pays the affiliate a commission for each lead they generate.

The business follows up with the lead

Once the lead is generated, the business will typically follow up with the customer to try to convert them into a paying customer. If the lead does convert into a sale, the affiliate may receive an additional commission.

How Does Pay-Per-Lead Affiliate Marketing Make Money?

Pay-per-lead affiliate marketing makes money by generating leads for businesses. As an affiliate, your job is to drive traffic to the business's website and encourage potential customers to provide their contact information. You are then paid a commission for each lead you generate, which can range from a few cents to several dollars or more depending on the industry and the business.

The key to making money with pay-per-lead affiliate marketing is to generate a high volume of quality leads. This requires a solid understanding of your target audience and the business's products or services. You'll need to create high-quality content, run targeted ads, and use other marketing channels to drive traffic to the business's website and encourage potential customers to provide their contact information.

Benefits of Pay-Per-Lead Affiliate Marketing

Pay-per-lead affiliate marketing offers many benefits to both affiliates and businesses. Here are some of the key benefits:

Cost-effective

PPL affiliate marketing is a cost-effective marketing strategy, as businesses only pay for actual leads.

Low risk

Since businesses only pay for actual leads, pay-per-lead affiliate marketing is a low-risk marketing strategy. Businesses don't have to worry about paying for traffic that doesn't convert into sales.

Passive income

Pay-per-lead affiliate marketing can be a great source of passive income for affiliates. Once you've created your content and set up your marketing channels, you can generate leads and earn commissions on autopilot.

Diversification

Pay-per-lead affiliate marketing allows affiliates to diversify their income streams by promoting multiple businesses at once.

Targeted marketing

By focusing on generating leads rather than sales, pay-per-lead affiliate marketing allows businesses to target their marketing efforts to a specific audience, which can improve conversion rates and ROI.

If you're interested in becoming a pay-per-lead affiliate marketer, here are some tips to help you succeed:

Choose the right niche

To succeed in pay-per-lead affiliate marketing, it's important to choose a niche that you're passionate about and that has a high demand for leads. Research the industry to determine what businesses are looking for leads and what types of offers are converting well.

Build a targeted audience

To generate quality leads, you need to have a targeted audience that is interested in the business's products or services. Build your audience through content marketing, social media, and other marketing channels that are relevant to your niche.

Create high-quality content

Your content should be informative, engaging, and relevant to your target audience. Create content that answers common questions or solves common problems that your target audience is experiencing.

Use multiple marketing channels

To generate a high volume of leads, you need to use multiple marketing channels. This may include content marketing, social media marketing, email marketing, and paid advertising.

Track your results

To improve your performance, it's important to track your results and make adjustments as needed. Use analytics tools to track your traffic, leads, and conversion rates, and make changes to your marketing strategy as needed.

Conclusion

Pay-per-lead affiliate marketing is a valuable source of passive income for affiliates who are able to generate a high volume of quality leads. By focusing on generating leads rather than sales, pay-per-lead affiliate marketing allows businesses to target their marketing efforts to a specific audience, which can improve conversion rates and ROI. To succeed in pay-per-lead affiliate marketing, it's important to choose the right niche, build a targeted audience, create high-quality content, use multiple marketing channels, and track your results. With the right strategy and approach, pay-per-lead affiliate marketing can be a highly effective way to generate passive income and diversify your income streams.

Chapter 4: Pay-Per-Click (PPC)

Pay-per-click (PPC) affiliate marketing is a popular method of affiliate marketing that allows affiliates to earn commissions by driving traffic to a business's website through paid advertising. In this chapter, we'll explore the basics of PPC affiliate marketing, how it works, and the benefits it offers to both affiliates and businesses.

Pay-per-click affiliate marketing is a type of affiliate marketing that pays affiliates a commission for each click they generate on a business's website through paid advertising. In other words, affiliates are paid for driving traffic to a business's website through paid search, display ads, or other forms of paid advertising.

How Does Pay-Per-Click Affiliate Marketing Work?

Pay-per-click affiliate marketing works by affiliates promoting a business's products or services through paid advertising. This can include paid search ads, display ads, or other forms of paid advertising.

When a user clicks on the affiliate's ad and is directed to the business's website, the affiliate earns a commission. The commission is usually a percentage of the sale, but it can also be a flat fee or a percentage of the click cost.

PPC affiliate marketing typically involves the use of affiliate networks, which act as intermediaries between affiliates and businesses. These networks provide affiliates with access to a wide range of businesses and products to promote, as well as tracking and reporting tools to monitor their performance.

Benefits of Pay-Per-Click Affiliate Marketing

High potential for earnings

Pay-per-click affiliate marketing can be a highly lucrative way to earn commissions, especially if you're able to generate a high volume of clicks that result in sales.

Control over ad spend

Affiliates have full control over their ad spend, which allows them to set budgets and optimize their campaigns for maximum ROI.

Access to a wide range of products

Pay-per-click affiliate marketing allows affiliates to promote a wide range of products from different businesses, which can help them diversify their income streams.

Scalability

PPC affiliate marketing is highly scalable, meaning that affiliates can increase their earnings by scaling up their advertising efforts.

Tracking and reporting

Affiliate networks provide affiliates with tracking and reporting tools to monitor their performance and make data-driven decisions to optimize their campaigns.

Tips for Succeeding in Pay-Per-Click Affiliate Marketing

If you're interested in succeeding in pay-per-click affiliate marketing, here are some tips to help you get started:

Choose the right niche

To succeed in pay-per-click affiliate marketing, it's important to choose a niche that you're passionate about and that has a high demand for the products or services you're promoting.

Use keyword research

Keyword research is critical for targeting the right audience and optimizing your ads for maximum ROI. Use keyword research tools to identify high-volume, low-competition keywords that are relevant to your niche.

Create high-quality ads

Your ads should be visually appealing, informative, and relevant to your target audience. Use compelling ad copy and high-quality images to attract clicks and generate leads.

Test and optimize

Testing and optimization are critical for maximizing your ROI in PPC affiliate marketing. Test different ad formats, targeting options, and bidding strategies to identify what works best for your campaigns.

Monitor your performance

Monitor your performance regularly and make data-driven decisions to optimize your campaigns. Use tracking and reporting tools to identify areas for improvement and make changes as needed.

Conclusion

Pay-per-click affiliate marketing is a valuable source of income for affiliates who are able to drive high-quality traffic to a business's website through paid advertising. With its high potential for earnings, control over ad spend, access to a wide range of products, scalability, and tracking and reporting tools, pay-per-click affiliate marketing is a popular and effective method of affiliate marketing. To succeed in pay-per-click affiliate marketing, it's important to choose the right niche, use keyword research, create high-quality ads, test and optimize, and monitor your performance regularly.

As with any form of affiliate marketing, success in pay-per-click affiliate marketing requires patience, dedication, and hard work. It may take time to build a profitable campaign, but with the right approach and a willingness to learn and adapt, it's possible to earn a significant income through PPC affiliate marketing.

In summary, pay-per-click affiliate marketing is a lucrative and flexible way to earn commissions by driving traffic to a business's website through paid advertising. By choosing the right niche, conducting keyword research, creating high-quality ads, testing and optimizing your campaigns, and monitoring your performance, you can maximize your ROI and build a profitable business as a pay-per-click affiliate marketer.

Chapter 5: Cost-Per-Action (CPA)

Cost-per-action (CPA) affiliate marketing is a performance-based marketing strategy where an affiliate is paid when a specific action is completed. In this chapter, we'll explore what cost-per-action affiliate marketing is, how it works, and the benefits it offers to affiliates and businesses.

Cost-per-action affiliate marketing is a type of affiliate marketing where the affiliate is paid when a specific action is completed, such as a sale, lead, or other conversion event. The affiliate earns a commission when a user completes the desired action on the business's website, such as making a purchase or filling out a form.

CPA affiliate marketing is different from traditional affiliate marketing in that the affiliate is not paid for clicks or impressions, but for actual conversions. This means that the business is only paying for results and is not taking on any risk.

How Does Cost-Per-Action Affiliate Marketing Work?

CPA affiliate marketing works by affiliates promoting a business's products or services and directing traffic to the business's website. When a user completes the desired action, such as making a purchase or filling out a form, the affiliate earns a commission.

The commission rate for CPA affiliate marketing can vary depending on the business and the desired action. For example, a business may pay a higher commission for a sale than for a lead.

CPA affiliate marketing typically involves the use of affiliate networks, which act as intermediaries between affiliates and businesses. These networks provide affiliates with access to a wide range of businesses and products to promote, as well as tracking and reporting tools to monitor their performance.

Benefits of Cost-Per-Action Affiliate Marketing

Low risk for businesses

Since businesses only pay for results, CPA affiliate marketing is a low-risk way to drive conversions and grow their business.

Control over the desired action

Businesses have full control over the desired action, which allows them to focus on the specific conversions that are most valuable to their business.

Easy to track and measure

CPA affiliate marketing is easy to track and measure, which allows businesses to monitor their ROI and make data-driven decisions to optimize their campaigns.

Access to a large pool of affiliates

Affiliate networks provide businesses with access to a large pool of affiliates, which can help them reach a wider audience and grow their business.

Flexibility

CPA affiliate marketing is a flexible way to grow a business, as businesses can set their desired action and commission rate to fit their specific goals and budget.

Tips for Succeeding in Cost-Per-Action Affiliate Marketing

If you're interested in succeeding in cost-per-action affiliate marketing, here are some tips to help you get started:

Choose the right niche

To succeed in CPA affiliate marketing, it's important to choose a niche that you're passionate about and that has a high demand for the products or services you're promoting.

Use targeted traffic sources

Use targeted traffic sources, such as search engine optimization, social media advertising, and email marketing, to drive high-quality traffic to the business's website.

Offer compelling incentives

Offer compelling incentives, such as discounts or free trials, to encourage users to complete the desired action.

Monitor your performance

Monitor your performance regularly and make data-driven decisions to optimize your campaigns. Use tracking and reporting tools to identify areas for improvement and make changes as needed.

Partner with the right businesses

Partner with businesses that have a good reputation and a track record of success in CPA affiliate marketing. Look for businesses that offer high commission rates and have a proven track record of converting traffic into leads or sales.

Conclusion

Cost-per-action affiliate marketing is a performance-based marketing strategy that offers benefits to both affiliates and businesses. With its low risk for businesses, control over the desired action, easy tracking and measurement, access to a large pool of affiliates, and flexibility, CPA affiliate marketing is a lucrative and flexible way to earn commissions.

Affiliates can benefit from CPA affiliate marketing by promoting high-converting offers and earning commissions on the actions completed by users they send to a business's website. CPA affiliate marketing offers affiliates the opportunity to earn more than they would with traditional affiliate marketing, as they are only paid for conversions, which can offer higher commission rates.

To succeed in cost-per-action affiliate marketing, it's important to choose the right niche, use targeted traffic sources, offer compelling incentives, monitor your performance, and partner with the right businesses. With these strategies, affiliates can maximize their ROI and build a profitable business in CPA affiliate marketing.

In summary, cost-per-action affiliate marketing is a performance-based marketing strategy where affiliates are paid for specific actions completed by users they send to a business's website. With its low risk for businesses, control over the desired action, easy tracking and measurement, access to a large pool of affiliates, and flexibility, CPA affiliate marketing is a lucrative and flexible way to earn commissions. By choosing the right niche, using targeted traffic sources, offering compelling incentives, monitoring performance, and partnering with the right businesses, affiliates can maximize their ROI and build a profitable business in CPA affiliate marketing.

Chapter 6: Revenue Sharing

Affiliate marketing has become one of the most popular ways for businesses to market their products or services. One of the common methods of affiliate marketing is the revenue sharing model, which is also known as the revenue sharing program or the revenue sharing affiliate model. In this chapter, we will explore what revenue sharing is and how it works in affiliate marketing.

Revenue sharing is a business model in which a business shares a percentage of the revenue it generates from a product or service with its partners. In affiliate marketing, revenue sharing involves sharing the revenue generated from sales made by affiliates. The revenue is usually shared in the form of a commission, which is paid to the affiliate for each sale they generate.

How Does Revenue Sharing Work in Affiliate Marketing?

In affiliate marketing, businesses set up a revenue sharing program, which is a way of compensating affiliates for generating sales. The revenue sharing program specifies the commission rate that affiliates will receive for each sale they generate. The commission rate can be a fixed amount or a percentage of the sale.

Affiliates sign up to the revenue sharing program and promote the business's products or services using their unique affiliate links. When a customer clicks on an affiliate link and makes a purchase, the sale is tracked, and the affiliate is credited with the commission. The commission is then paid out to the affiliate, usually on a monthly basis.

Benefits of Revenue Sharing in Affiliate Marketing

Revenue sharing in affiliate marketing offers several benefits to businesses and affiliates. For businesses, revenue sharing allows them to expand their reach and increase their sales without having to invest in advertising. They only pay commissions on actual sales generated by affiliates, which means there is no upfront cost to join the program.

For affiliates, revenue sharing allows them to earn a passive income by promoting products or services they believe in. Affiliates can earn commissions on every sale they generate, and there is no limit to the amount they can earn. They also have the flexibility to promote products or services that are relevant to their audience.

Challenges of Revenue Sharing in Affiliate Marketing

While revenue sharing can be a beneficial model for both businesses and affiliates, it can also present some challenges. One of the challenges is tracking sales and ensuring that affiliates are paid the correct commission.

Businesses need to have a reliable tracking system in place to ensure that they are tracking all sales generated by affiliates and paying the correct commission.

Another challenge is the potential for fraudulent activity. Some affiliates may use unethical methods to generate sales, such as using fake leads or spamming customers. Businesses need to have a system in place to detect and prevent fraudulent activity and ensure that they are only paying commissions on legitimate sales.

Conclusion

Revenue sharing is a popular model in affiliate marketing that allows businesses to expand their reach and increase sales without investing in advertising. Affiliates can earn a passive income by promoting products or services they believe in, and there is no limit to the amount they can earn. However, businesses need to have a reliable tracking system in place to ensure that affiliates are paid the correct commission, and they need to take steps to prevent fraudulent activity. With the right system and procedures in place, revenue sharing can be a beneficial model for both businesses and affiliates in affiliate marketing.

Chapter 7: Cost-Per-Impression (CPM)

Cost per impression, also known as cost per thousand impressions (CPM), is a pricing model used in online advertising, where an advertiser pays a fee for every 1,000 times an ad is displayed to a user. The cost per impression is based on the number of impressions, regardless of whether the user clicks on the ad or takes any other action.

How Does CPM Work in Affiliate Marketing?

In affiliate marketing, the CPM model is used to compensate affiliates for the number of impressions they generate for a particular ad. The affiliate is paid a fee based on the number of times the ad is displayed to a user, regardless of whether the user clicks on the ad or takes any other action.

To implement the CPM model in affiliate marketing, the business sets up an affiliate program that includes the CPM pricing model. Affiliates sign up for the program and are provided with a unique link or banner to promote the business's products or services.

When a user clicks on the affiliate link or banner, they are taken to the business's website, and the ad is displayed to the user. The ad is tracked by the affiliate program, and the affiliate is credited with an impression. The affiliate is paid a fee for every 1,000 impressions generated by their promotions.

Benefits of CPM in Affiliate Marketing

The CPM model has several benefits for businesses and affiliates. For businesses, CPM is a cost-effective way to increase their brand awareness and promote their products or services without having to pay for clicks or other actions. The business only pays for impressions, regardless of whether the user takes any other action. This can be particularly useful for businesses that are focused on brand awareness and need to reach a large number of users.

For affiliates, CPM offers a predictable revenue stream. Affiliates are paid a fee for every 1,000 impressions generated by their promotions, regardless of whether the user clicks on the ad or takes any other action. This means that affiliates can earn a commission for every impression they generate, even if the user does not make a purchase.

Challenges of CPM in Affiliate Marketing

One of the challenges of the CPM model is that it is difficult to track and measure the effectiveness of the ad. Unlike the pay-per-click model, where the advertiser only pays for clicks, the CPM model does not take into account whether the user takes any other action. This can make it difficult to determine the ROI of the ad and whether it is generating the desired results.

Another challenge of the CPM model is that it may not be suitable for all types of businesses or products. CPM is most effective for businesses that are focused on brand awareness and need to reach a large number of users. It may not be as effective for businesses that are focused on generating sales or leads.

Conclusion

The cost per impression model is a popular pricing model used in online advertising, and it is also used in affiliate marketing. CPM is a cost-effective way for businesses to promote their products or services and increase their brand awareness without having to pay for clicks or other actions. Affiliates can earn a commission for every impression they generate, providing a predictable revenue stream. However, the CPM model may not be suitable for all types of businesses or products, and it can be difficult to track the effectiveness of the ad. As with any marketing strategy, businesses and affiliates need to consider the pros and cons of the CPM model before implementing it in their affiliate marketing strategy.

To make the most of the CPM model in affiliate marketing, businesses need to choose their affiliates carefully. They should select affiliates who have a strong following in their target audience and who can generate a large number of impressions. Additionally, they should monitor the performance of their ads and adjust their campaigns accordingly to ensure they are generating the desired results.

Affiliates also need to be strategic when using the CPM model. They should promote products or services that are likely to generate a large number of impressions, and they should use channels that are most effective at reaching their target audience. They should also be transparent with their followers and disclose that they are promoting a product or service in exchange for a fee.

In conclusion, the CPM model is a valuable method for businesses and affiliates to increase brand awareness and generate revenue in affiliate marketing. While it may not be suitable for all types of businesses or products, it can be a cost-effective way to promote products or services and generate a predictable revenue stream. With the right strategy and careful planning, businesses and affiliates can make the most of the CPM model and achieve their marketing goals.

www.ingramcontent.com/pod-product-compliance
Lightning Source LLC
Chambersburg PA
CBHW071146220526
45467CB00015B/2045